Jesus
is the
Great Physician:
The True Story of a Miraculous Healing

ANDREA SPIESS

AuthorHouse™
1663 Liberty Drive
Bloomington, IN 47403
www.authorhouse.com
Phone: 833-262-8899

ISBN: 979-8-8230-2123-4 (sc)
ISBN: 979-8-8230-2125-8 (hc)
ISBN: 979-8-8230-2124-1 (e)

Library of Congress Control Number: 2024901853

Print information available on the last page.

Published by AuthorHouse 01/30/2024

authorHOUSE®

"The thief comes only to steal and kill and destroy. I came that they may have life and have it abundantly."
John 10:10 American Standard Version

I dedicate this book back to Jesus, the original author of this story. I declare that this book is an altar of the Lord. Let all who come across this book receive healing and begin the process of turning their faith into miracles.

There is a little girl named Kenzie Joelle.
She's a free-spirited child with a story to tell.
Everything about this story is true.
Her miraculous healing, now shared with you.

First, here's a bit about Kenzie Jo.
She doesn't say much. She's mostly on the go.
She loves climbing, jumping, and making a mess.
She loves puppies, turtles, and wearing a dress.

Kenzie's heart is made of the purest of gold,
And while she is shy, she's also quite bold.
Her special way to show love to her crew,
Is by saying the words, "I super love you."

Before she was healed, she would get very ill.
Her knees would ache with a fever and chill.
Her body didn't work the way that it should.
She was sick, ouchie, and didn't feel good.

On her bad days, she was stuck in her bed,
Few words spoken and a smile slow to spread.
Her joints all hurt and her ankles would swell.
As months went on, she still felt unwell.

Doctor appointments, medicine, and shots,
Blood draws that left her stomach in knots.
No solutions came from treatments and tests,
Kenzie hardly felt her best.

As the years passed by, her family all prayed,
And believed that the Lord would heal her one day.

One night when Kenzie was sleeping in bed,
Her mother snuck in and laid hands on her head.
A declaration of healing was long overdue.
And with big faith, her momma just knew-
Jesus can heal anyone, anywhere.
Because of that, Kenzie's mother declared,
"She IS healed by Jesus, Lord over all,
Who loves His people, especially the small.
For it is His will to take all the pain,
All sickness, sorrow, worry, and shame."

"And Devil," her mother said a bit riled,
"You get your hands off of God's child."

Kenzie's mother believed a difference was made.
Prayer is powerful when faith is displayed.

In this story, this is when things get good.
When Jesus steps in, it's just understood,
He makes things better. He makes everyone shine.
He makes all things good in His perfect time.

Three days later, after the prayer from her mother,
A day that seemed just like any other,
Until suddenly, Kenzie looked up to say,
"Jesus woke me up today."

Addy, her sister, who she was playing with,
Looked at Kenzie thinking this was a myth.
Kenzie began sharing, confident and calm.
Then Addy said, "Wait! Let's go tell our mom!"

They found Mom in a room folding some jeans,
Never suspecting what this day would mean.
Addy said, "Mom, you need to hear this.
Kenzie has something you won't want to miss."

So Kenzie began to share her encounter.
In her bed is where Jesus had found her...

He glowed with light and a smile on His face.
He wore a white robe and a sash on His waist.
He had brown hair and eyes that were tender,
And strong arms that showed He was a defender.

He had wounds on His hands, feet, and forehead,
Revealing that some of His blood had been shed.
His look of perfect love made it quite clear,
That Kenzie had nothing at all to fear.

He scooped her up and gave her a hug,
Then took her hand and gave it a tug.
It's time to go, but there's no need to worry.
No time to waste, but also no hurry.

A bright scene appeared before Kenzie's eyes.
She knew she was in heavenly skies.

He showed her some pets who had passed away,
And explained that Heaven is where animals stay.
He showed her a bird that was flying around.
The bird she had prayed for when it fell to the ground.

"The bird is okay now," Jesus revealed.
"Animals come here when it's time to be healed."

Then Jesus leaned down and touched her chest,
"I live in here. That's why you're blessed."
"I super love you," He said like a song.
And that's how she knew He was there all along.

Jesus continued with perfect design,
"You are special because you are mine."

Then Jesus, who is the Great Physician,
Checked her joints with perfect precision.
Her ankles, her knees, her elbows as well,
Her fingers, her toes, wherever she swelled.

Looking pleased, He gave Kenzie a hug.
Then took her hand with one final tug.
As Kenzie traveled back to her bed,
A new joy in her heart began to spread.

Kenzie's mom gasped at what was just shared,
Remembering in faith what she had declared.
"Kenzie, did He take your ouchies away?"
"He did, Mommy. Now can I go and play?"

"Daddy, get in here!" Her mother called out.
"Jesus healed Kenzie and I have no doubt!"
So Kenzie shared once more with her daddy.
Tears of joy were shed by her mom, dad, and Addy.

The version of Kenzie who struggled before,
Now giggles, sings, and smiles a lot more.
With a strong body and joy in her heart,
Jesus gave Kenzie a new life to start.

As others were told and the story was shared,
More people found out how much Jesus cared.
It became a reminder to all who would hear,
That Jesus still heals those He holds dear.

All the ouchies, pain, illness, and tears,
Bad dreams, sorrow, and all of the fears,
Are not things you have to face all alone.
Trust in the one who is on the throne.

Join God's Family

Jesus loves us, and He wants you to know,
That He is with you wherever you go.
He is worthy of your trust and your love.
He can do big things you never thought of.

For by His ouchies, we can be healed.
You are God's child, and that's a big deal.
Perhaps it's time to ask Him into your heart,
So He can begin to set you apart.

Dear Jesus,

I know sometimes I do things that I shouldn't do. But you came to earth, died on the cross, and rose from the dead because you love me so much. Thank you for loving and forgiving me for my mistakes, whether I realized they were sins or not. Help me do what you want me to, and follow you with all my heart. I want you to be part of my life forever. So come live in my heart and make me just like you.

In Jesus' name, I pray.

Amen.

Congratulations, you're in God's family now!
Dance, jump around, shout it out, take a bow!
And reach out to us so we can celebrate the day,
You asked Jesus in your heart and sent the enemy away.

Always remember who Jesus is,
He brings life, and hope, and everything is His.
And if you need the Great Physician,
You just put yourself in the perfect position.

Dear Reader,

As a testament to our good God, this book was written a year after my daughter, Kenzie, was miraculously healed from systemic juvenile idiopathic arthritis (SJIA).

Years of watching my child struggle with frequent illnesses, arthritic flare-ups, surgeries, echocardiograms, and blood draws created a desire to learn about the true authority we have in Jesus. Three days after declaring my child healed under the blood of Jesus, our four-year-old had her miraculous encounter shared in this book.

The changes we noticed in Kenzie were immediate. Her swelling and flare-ups ceased, and her overall stamina, speed, and agility drastically improved.

Our child, who was sick every other week, went four months before even contracting the common cold after her healing encounter. The greatest change of all was Kenzie's new love for Jesus. She continues to share that her favorite part of her experience was the healing hug from our Lord.

Whether you desire to teach your child about our God who heals, or you are currently seeking Him for such a miracle, I believe this book was placed before you divinely. We declare in faith that a miracle touches your household today in Jesus' name! And we say, *Devil, you get your hands off of God's children.*

May God bless you and your family.

Sincerely,

Andrea Spiess
turningfaithintomiracles.com
faithtomiracles@gmail.com

- A Prayer of Authority for Parents -

Heavenly Father, in Jesus' name,

I am a sinner in need of a Savior[1], and I repent for settling for the lies of this world. Lies that You don't do miracles today.[2] Lies that You don't hear me when I pray.[3] Lies that You can heal, but You won't.[4] These lies do not align with who You are.

Lord, I lay my doubt at Your feet and ask for mountain-moving faith.[5] Please give me the same faith as the woman who knew that all she needed was to touch the border of Your garment to receive her healing.[6]

Lord, I am reaching out to You now asking for a miracle for my child that only You can do. You know all the suffering my child has endured at the hands of the enemy.[7] Today, as an act of faith, I come into agreement with Your perfect will for his/her life.

In Jesus' name, I take all power and authority over the power of the enemy.[8] I rebuke the enemy's attacks against my child, and I call down any plots, schemes, and plans of the enemy. *DEVIL, YOU GET YOUR HANDS OFF MY CHILD IN JESUS' NAME.* I break every lie, curse, demonic attack, and affliction that has come against my child, and I cover him/her with the blood of Jesus.[9] I declare perfect health (body, mind, soul, and emotions) over my child.[10] I declare and decree that whatever has been stolen from my child and our family must be restored sevenfold in Jesus' name.[11]

Lord, I thank You that You are good. I thank You for Your promises.[12] I thank You that Your sacrifice at the cross is now my victory.[13] And I thank You that Your goodness and Your love endures forever.[14]

In Jesus' name, I pray. Amen.

<u>Biblical References</u>

(1) Romans 3:23

(2) James 1:17

(3) 1 John 5:15

(4) Jeremiah 29:11

(5) Matthew 17:20

(6) Luke 8:43-44

(7) John 10:10

(8) 1 John 4:4

(9) Hebrews 2:14

(10) 1 Peter 2:24

(11) Proverbs 6:31

(12) 2 Peter 1:3

(13) 1 Corinthians 15:57

(14) Psalm 136:1

Printed in the United States
by Baker & Taylor Publisher Services